B... Quotes & Facts

By Blago Kirov

First Edition

*****

Bernard Shaw: Quotes & Facts
*****

Foreword

"I often quote myself. It adds spice to my conversation."

This book is an anthology of 217 quotes from George Bernard Shaw and 73 selected facts about George Bernard Shaw.

George Bernard Shaw receives a Nobel Prize for Literature 1925.

Between 1879 and 1883 George Bernard Shaw earned only £6 from his writings.

His wife Charlotte resolved to have no children and abstained from sex completely throughout the marriage.

As a music critic, George Bernard Shaw championed the German composer Richard Wagner.

George Bernard Shaw is the only person to have been awarded both a Nobel Prize for Literature (1925) and an Oscar (1938) for work on transcribing Pygmalion (adaptation of his play of the same name).

At the age of 16, George Bernard Shaw lived through the breakup of his parent's marriage, as his mother left to live with her singing coach. Shaw stayed with his father.

Shaw actually hated the George in his name, and used just Bernard Shaw.

George Bernard Shaw was known to dislike aristocrats and nobleman. One time he received invitation from local lord stating: "Lord C. Will be home Tuesday between 4 and 6". Bernard Shaw returned invitation and wrote down: "George Bernard Shaw too".

Shaw's views on sex, marriage, and domestic bliss stemmed from his seduction, at 29, by Jenny Paterson, a woman he later described as "sexually insatiable."

George Bernard Shaw was a vegetarian.

"I'm an atheist and I thank God for it."

"Lack of money is the root of all evil."

"Never wrestle with pigs. You both get dirty and the pig likes it."

"There are two tragedies in life. One is to lose your heart's desire. The other is to gain it."

"The English are not a very spiritual people, so they invented cricket to give them some idea of eternity."

"A book is like a child: it is easier to bring it into the world than to control it when it is launched there."

"A fashion is nothing but an induced epidemic."

"A fool's brain digests philosophy into folly, science into superstition, and art into pedantry. Hence University education."

"A gentleman is one who puts more into the world than he takes out."

"A government which robs Peter to pay Paul can always depend on the support of Paul."

"A happy family is but an earlier heaven."

"A learned man is an idler who kills time by study."

Some Facts about George Bernard Shaw

George Bernard Shaw was born on July 26, 1856.

George Bernard Shaw appears on sleeve of The Beatles' "Sgt Pepper's Lonely Hearts Club".

George Bernard Shaw is the great uncle of author, actor and filmmaker Scott Shaw.

In 1879 George Bernard Shaw joined the Zetetical Society, a club devoted to discussions of evolution, atheism, and other topics engaging the interest of intellectual circles at the time.

George Bernard Shaw was known for his wit, it even led to creation of a Shawism - witty phrase.

In 1882 George Bernard Shaw read part of Capital, by the German revolutionist Karl Marx, and became a socialist.

Shaw's father once visited a Dublin surgeon to try and get his eye squint corrected. That surgeon happened to be the very successful father of Oscar Wilde. The treatment was not successful.

Until 1933 George Bernard Shaw was a frequent lecturer in behalf of socialism, and socialist ideas were central in much of his writing.

George Bernard Shaw often stood on a box in the speaker's corner of London's Hyde Park to hold forth on his socialist political views.

George Bernard Shaw first gained a reputation in the esthetic field as a music and drama critic.

As a drama critic, George Bernard Shaw crusaded for the Norwegian playwright Henrik Ibsen and attacked the Shakespearean productions of the British actor and theatrical manager Sir Henry Irving.

George Bernard Shaw was art critic for The World in 1886-87; music critic for The Star, under the pseudonym "Como di Bassetto", from 1888 to 1890; music critic for The World from 1890 to 1894: and drama critic for The Saturday Review from 1895 to 1898.

In his letters to the British actress Dame Ellen Alice Terry, Shaw attempted to win her support for the new theater of ideas.

George Bernard Shaw joined the Fabian Society, a socialist club, in 1884, was elected almost immediately to its executive committee, and served in it until 1911.

George Bernard Shaw brought into the Fabian Society his personal friend the British economist, writer, and social reformer Sidney James Webb, who became a leading socialist writer.

Through Sidney James Webb and his wife Beatrice, George Bernard Shaw met Charlotte Payne-Townshend, an Irish heiress and Fabian, who became his wife.

George Bernard Shaw edited and contributed to Fabian Essays in Socialism (1889), an anthology generally considered a classic of socialist literature.

George Bernard Shaw married but it was never consummated and he had no children.

In his youth Shaw enrolled successively in four schools.

George Bernard Shaw receives a Nobel Prize for Literature 1925.

Between 1879 and 1883 George Bernard Shaw earned only £6 from his writings.

His wife Charlotte resolved to have no children and abstained from sex completely throughout the marriage.

As a music critic, George Bernard Shaw championed the German composer Richard Wagner.

George Bernard Shaw is the only person to have been awarded both a Nobel Prize for Literature (1925) and an Oscar (1938) for work on transcribing Pygmalion (adaptation of his play of the same name).

At the age of 16, George Bernard Shaw lived through the breakup of his parent's marriage, as his mother left to live with her singing coach. Shaw stayed with his father.

Shaw actually hated the George in his name, and used just Bernard Shaw.

George Bernard Shaw was known to dislike aristocrats and nobleman. One time he received invitation from local lord stating: "Lord C. Will be home Tuesday between 4 and 6". Bernard Shaw returned invitation and wrote down: "George Bernard Shaw too".

Shaw's views on sex, marriage, and domestic bliss stemmed from his seduction, at 29, by Jenny Paterson, a woman he later described as "sexually insatiable."

George Bernard Shaw was a vegetarian.

His father, George Carr Shaw, was an unsuccessful businessman; his mother, Lucinda Elizabeth Gurley, was a music teacher.

George Bernard Shaw refused to sell the screen rights to his plays, but would only license them for renewable five-year periods.

George Bernard Shaw supervised, wrote the screenplays for, and had creative control over three film versions of his plays-- the "Pygmalion", the "Major Barbara", and the "Caesar and Cleopatra".

George Bernard Shaw was Opponent of First World War.

George Bernard Shaw obtained a clerical Job in a Dublin real-estate office in 1871. Although he found the work stultifying, he remained with the firm four and a half years.

George Bernard Shaw was a keen amateur photographer.

George Bernard Shaw was also an essayist, novelist and short story writer.

Issues which engaged Shaw's attention included education, marriage, religion, government, health care, and class privilege.

When George Orwell asked George Bernard Shaw for permission to quote from one of his works in a BBC interview for the 'Voice', magazine program, to be broadcast by the Indian Service Shaw responded with the brief refusal "I veto it ruthlessly".

George Bernard Shaw was supported belief in Eugenics.

Despite nearly dieing from smallpox, Shaw joined a public campaign in opposition to vaccination against smallpox.

When his house at Ayot St Lawrence became a museum his Oscar statuette was so tarnished the curator, believing it had no value, used it as a door stop.

With Sidney and Beatrice Webb, and Graham Wallas, George Bernard Shaw was a co-founder of the London School of Economics.

George Bernard Shaw was a leading member of the Fabian society.

George Bernard Shaw was supporter of Salvation Army ideas.

In George Orwell's Animal Farm, Mr. Whymper a man hired by Napoleon to represent Animal Farm in human society, is loosely based on George Bernard Shaw who visited the U.S.S.R. in 1931 and praised Stalin and what he found.

His marriage to Irish heiress, Charlotte Payne-Townshend, felt the Paterson aftershock, when Shaw spent his honeymoon in 1898 writing the anti-romantic Caesar and Cleopatra.

George Bernard Shaw used the pseudonyms "GBS" and "Corno di Bassetto" as a columnist.

George Bernard Shaw was an iconoclastic playwright, journalist, polemicist, scintillating public speaker, arts reviewer and campaigning socialist.

George Bernard Shaw had no particular religion, but was receptive to a range of religious views.

George Bernard Shaw was a loud critic of contemporary education. In his Treatise on Parents and Children he considered the curriculum useless.

George Bernard Shaw telegrammed Winston Churchill just prior to the opening of Major Barbara: "Have reserved two tickets for first night. Come and bring a friend if you have one." Churchill wired back, "Impossible to come to first night. Will come to second night, if you have one."

George Bernard Shaw rejected many honors during his lifetime. He only accepted the Nobel Prize at the behest of his wife who thought it would bring honor to Ireland.

Of Shaw's more than 50 plays, none achieved greater unexpected success than Pygmalion. Adapted for the New York stage in 1956 as My Fair Lady, starring Julie Andrews, the play broke Broadway records in its long run.

George Bernard Shaw and his wife were vacationing at an English seaside resort when someone told them that Harpo Marx was nude-sunbathing, down on the beach. Shaw and his wife immediately went to the beach and surprised Marx in the act. This began their long friendship.

His will left a small fortune to be used to develop a precise English alphabet of 40 letters to replace the current one.

George Bernard Shaw wrote five novels, all of which were rejected, before finding his first success as a music critic on the Star newspaper.

George Bernard Shaw served as a local councilor in the St Pancras district of London for several years from 1897.

Shaw's correspondence with Mrs. Patrick Campbell was adapted for the stage by Jerome Kilty as Dear Liar: A Comedy of Letters.

Richard Wagner was a source of inspiration for George Bernard Shaw.

Shaw's letters to prominent actress Ellen Terry have also been published and dramatized.

George Bernard Shaw was friends with Isadora Duncan,a famous dancer.

George Bernard Shaw grew up with a lifelong animosity towards school teachers and the academic system.

George Bernard Shaw never consummated his marriage with Charlotte Payne-Townshend, but did have numerous affairs with other married women.

The National Gallery of Ireland received a substantial donation from Shaw's will.

From 1906 until his death in 1950, George Bernard Shaw lived at Shaw's Corner in the small village of Ayot St Lawrence, Hertfordshire.

George Bernard Shaw had a long time friendship with Gilbert Keith Chesterton, the Catholic writer, and there are many humourous stories about their complicated relationship.

Despite the fact that he was a democratic socialist, in the 1930s George Bernard Shaw approved of the dictatorship of Stalin and even made some ambiguous statements that could be interpreted as being pro-Hitler.

In 1895, George Bernard Shaw became the drama critic of the Saturday Review, and this was the first step in his progress towards a lifetime's work as a dramatist.

A characteristic of Shaw's published plays is the lengthy prefaces that accompany them. In these essays, Shaw wrote more about his usually controversial opinions on the issues touched by the plays than about the plays themselves. Some prefaces are much longer than the actual play.

At 67, Shaw wrote Saint Joan, thought by many admirers to be his greatest effort.

At 91, still creative, George Bernard Shaw finished Buoyant Billions and promptly began a new comedy, working in a one-room hut he called "The Shelter."

George Bernard Shaw died at an age of 94 when he fell down the ladder while trimming a tree.

His Words

"I often quote myself. It adds spice to my conversation."

"I'm an atheist and I thank God for it."

"Lack of money is the root of all evil."

"Never wrestle with pigs. You both get dirty and the pig likes it."

"There are two tragedies in life. One is to lose your heart's desire. The other is to gain it."

"The English are not a very spiritual people, so they invented cricket to give them some idea of eternity."

"A book is like a child: it is easier to bring it into the world than to control it when it is launched there."

"A fashion is nothing but an induced epidemic."

"A fool's brain digests philosophy into folly, science into superstition, and art into pedantry. Hence University education."

"A gentleman is one who puts more into the world than he takes out."

"A government which robs Peter to pay Paul can always depend on the support of Paul."

"A happy family is but an earlier heaven."

"A learned man is an idler who kills time by study."

"A life spent making mistakes is not only more honorable, but more useful than a life spent doing nothing."

"A man learns to skate by staggering about making a fool of himself. Indeed, he progresses in all things by resolutely making a fool of himself."

"A man of great common sense and good taste - meaning thereby a man without originality or moral courage. "

"A miracle, my friend, is an event which creates faith."

"A Native American elder once described his own inner struggles in this manner: Inside of me there are two dogs. One of the dogs is mean and evil. The other dog is good. The mean dog fights the good dog all the time. When asked which dog wins, he reflected for a moment and replied, The one I feed the most."

"A pessimist is a man who thinks everybody is as nasty as himself, and hates them for it."

"A photographer is like a cod, which produces a million eggs in order that one may reach maturity."

"After all, the wrong road always leads somewhere."

"Alcohol is the anesthesia by which we endure the operation of life."

"All censorships exist to prevent anyone from challenging current conceptions and existing institutions. All progress is initiated by challenging current conceptions, and executed by supplanting existing institutions. Consequently, the first condition of progress is the removal of censorship."

"All great truths begin as blasphemies."

"An asylum for the sane would be empty in America."

"An Irishman's heart is nothing but his imagination."

"Animals are my friends...and I don't eat my friends."

"As long as I have a want, I have a reason for living. Satisfaction is death. "

"Assassination is the extreme form of censorship."

"Atrocities are not less atrocities when they occur in laboratories and are called medical research."

"Bear it like a man, even if you feel it like an ass. "

"Better keep yourself clean and bright; you are the window through which you must see the world."

"Beware of false knowledge; it is more dangerous than ignorance."

"Both optimists and pessimists contribute to society. The optimist invents the aeroplane, the pessimist the parachute."

"But to admire a strong person; and to live under that strong person's thumb are; two different things."

"Censorship ends in logical completeness when nobody is allowed to read any books except the books that nobody reads."

"Choose silence of all virtues, for by it you hear other men's imperfections, and conceal your own."

"Confusing monogamy with morality has done more to destroy the conscience of the human race than any other error."

"Criminals do not die by the hands of the law. They die by the hands of other men."

"Custom will reconcile people to any atrocity, and fashion will drive them to acquire any custom."

"Dancing is a perpendicular expression of a horizontal desire."

"Decency cannot be discussed without indecency!"

"Democracy is a device that ensures we shall be governed no better than we deserve."

"Do not do unto others as you would that they should do unto you. Their tastes may not be the same."

"Do not waste your time on Social Questions. What is the matter with the poor is Poverty what is the matter with the rich is Uselessness."

"Do you think that the things people make fools of themselves about are any less real and true than the things they behave sensibly about? They are more true: they are the only things that are true."

"Doing what needs to be done may not make you happy, but it will make you great."

"Don't think you can frighten me by telling me that I am alone. France is alone. God is alone. And the loneliness of God is His strength."

"England and America are two countries separated by the same language."

"Everything happens to everybody sooner or later if there is time enough."

"Few people think more than two or three times a year; I have made an international reputation for myself by thinking once or twice a week."

"First love is only a little foolishness and a lot of curiosity."

"For four wicked centuries the world has dreamed this foolish dream of efficiency; and the end is not yet. But the end will come."

"Forgive him, for he believes that the customs of his tribe are the laws of nature!"

"Get out of my way; for I won't stop for you."

"Happy is the man who can make a living by his hobby"

"Hatred is the coward's revenge for being intimidated."

"He knows nothing; and he thinks he knows everything. That points clearly to a political career."

"He who can, does. He who cannot, teaches. "

"He who has never hoped can never despair"

"Heaven, as conventionally conceived, is a place so inane, so dull, so useless, so miserable that nobody has ever ventured to describe a whole day in heaven, though plenty of people have described a day at the seaside."

"Hell is full of musical amateurs: music is the brandy of the damned. May not one lost soul be permitted to abstain?"

"Hell, they says, is paved with good intentions."

"I am afraid we must make the world honest before we can honestly say to our children that honesty is the best policy."

"I am enclosing two tickets to the first night of my new play; bring a friend ... if you have one."

"I am of the opinion that my life belongs to the community, and as long as I live, it is my privilege to do for it whatever I can. I want to be thoroughly used up when I die, for the harder I work, the more I live. Life is no 'brief candle' to me. It ia a sort of splendid torch which I have got hold of for a moment, and I want to make it burn as brightly as possible before handing it on to the future generations."

"I am sorry to have to introduce the subject of Christmas. It is an indecent subject; a cruel, gluttonous subject; a drunken, disorderly subject; a wasteful, disastrous subject; a wicked, cadging, lying, filthy, blasphemous and demoralizing subject. Christmas is forced on a reluctant and disgusted nation by the shopkeepers and the press: on its own merits it would wither and shrivel in the fiery breath of universal hatred; and anyone who looked back to it would be turned into a pillar of greasy sausages. "

"I can't turn your soul on. Leave me those feelings; and you can take away the voice and the face. They are not you."

"I choose not to make a graveyard of my body for the rotting corpses of dead animals."

"I dislike feeling at home when I am abroad."

"I do not know what I think until I write it."

"I don't know if there are men on the moon, but if there are they must be using the earth as their lunatic asylum"

"I finished my first book seventy-six years ago. I offered it to every publisher on the English-speaking earth I had ever heard of. Their refusals were unanimous: and it did not get into print until, fifty years later; publishers would publish anything that had my name on it."

"I have defined the hundred per cent American as ninety-nine per cent an idiot."

"I have my own soul. My own spark of divine fire."

"I have never thought much of the courage of a lion tamer. Inside the cage he is at least safe from other men. There is not much harm in a lion. He has no ideals, no religion, no politics, no chivalry, no gentility; in short, no reason for destroying anything that he does not want to eat"

"I knew if I waited around long enough something like this would happen."

"I learned long ago, never to wrestle with a pig, you get dirty; and besides, the pig likes it."

"I like flowers, I also like children, but I do not chop their heads off and keep them in bowls of water around the house."

"I never resist temptation because I have found that things that are bad for me do not tempt me."

"I try to follow his example, not to imitate him."

"I want to be thoroughly used up when I die for the harder I work the more I live. I rejoice in life for its own sake."

"I'm not a teacher: only a fellow traveler of whom you asked the way. I pointed ahead - ahead of myself as well as you."

"If any religion had a chance of ruling over England, nay Europe within the next hundred years, it could be Islam."

"If history repeats itself, and the unexpected always happens, how incapable must Man be of learning from experience."

"If you can't get rid of the skeleton in your closet, you'd best teach it to dance."

"If you can't appreciate what you've got, you'd better get what you can appreciate."

"If you cannot get rid of the family skeleton, you may as well make it dance."

"If you have an apple and I have an apple and we exchange these apples then you and I will still each have one apple. But if you have an idea and I have an idea and we exchange these ideas, then each of us will have two ideas."

"If you take too long in deciding what to do with your life, you'll find you've done it."

"If you teach a man anything, he will never learn."

"Imagination is the beginning of creation. You imagine what you desire, you will what you imagine and at last you create what you will."

"Imitation is not just the sincerest form of flattery - it's the sincerest form of learning."

"In an ugly and unhappy world the richest man can purchase nothing but ugliness and unhappiness."

"In heaven an angel is no one in particular."

"In literature the ambition of the novice is to acquire the literary language; the struggle of the adept is to get rid of it."

"Independence? That's middle class blasphemy. We are all dependent on one another, every soul of us on earth."

"It is a curious sensation: the sort of pain that goes mercifully beyond our powers of feeling. When your heart is broken, your boats are burned: nothing matters any more. It is the end of happiness and the beginning of peace."

"It is a woman's business to get married as soon as possible, and a man's

"It is dangerous to be sincere unless you are also stupid."

"It is not pleasure that makes life worth living. It is life that makes pleasure worth having."

"It's all that the young can do for the old, to shock them and keep them up to date."

"Liberty means responsibility. That is why most men dread it."

"Life does not cease to be funny when people die any more than it ceases to be serious when people laugh."

"Life is like a flame that is always burning itself out..."

"Life is no brief candle to me. It is a sort of splendid torch which I have got a hold of for the moment, and I want to make it burn as brightly as possible before handing it on to future generations."

"Life is not meant to be easy, my child; but take courage: it can be delightful."

"Life isn't about finding yourself. Life is about creating yourself."

"Like all young men, you greatly exaggerate the difference between one young woman and another."

"Make it a rule never to give a child a book you would not read yourself."

"Marriage is an alliance entered into by a man who can't sleep with the window shut, and a woman who can't sleep with the window open."

"Marriage is to me apostasy, profanation of the sanctuary of my soul, violation of my manhood, sale of my birthright, shameful surrender, ignominious capitulation, acceptance of defeat."

"Martyrdom, sir, is what these people like: it is the only way in which a man can become famous without ability."

"Men are wise in proportion, not to their experience, but to their capacity for experience."

"Morals are a luxury of the rich."

"Most people go to their grave with their music inside them."

"My main reason for adopting literature as a profession was that, as the author is never seen by his clients, he need not dress respectably."

"My method is to take the utmost trouble to find the right thing to say, and then to say it with the utmost levity."

"My way of joking is to tell the truth. It's the funniest joke in the world."

"Never waste jealousy on a real man: it is the imaginary man that supplants us all in the long run."

"No man ever believes that the Bible means what it says: He is always convinced that it says what he means."

"No use slaving for me and then saying you want to be cared for: who cares for a slave? If you come back, come back for the sake of good fellowship; for you'll get nothing else."

"Oh, well, if you want original conversations, you'd better go and talk to yourself."

"One man that has a mind and knows it can always beat ten men who haven't and don't."

"Only in books has mankind known perfect truth, love and beauty."

"Only on paper has humanity yet achieved glory, beauty, truth, knowledge, virtue, and abiding love."

"Pasteboard pies and paper flowers are being banished from the stage by the growth of that power of accurate observation which is commonly called cynicism by those who have not got it...."

"Patriotism is, fundamentally, a conviction that a particular country is the best in the world because you were born in it...."

"People are always blaming their circumstances for what they are. I don't believe in circumstances. The people who get on in this world are the people who get up and look for the circumstances they want, and if they can't find them, make them."

"People who say it cannot be done should not interrupt those who are doing it."

"Physically there is nothing to distinguish human society from the farm-yard except that children are more troublesome and costly than chickens and calves and that men and women are not so completely enslaved as farm stock."

"Power does not corrupt men; fools, however, if they get into a position of power, corrupt power."

"Progress is impossible without change; and those who cannot change their minds cannot change anything."

"Reading made Don Quixote a gentleman. Believing what he read made him mad."

"Science never solves a problem without creating ten more"

"Set me anything to do as a task, and it is inconceivable the desire I have to do something else."

"Shall I turn up the light for you?

"She had lost the art of conversation, but not, unfortunately, the power of speech."

"Silence is the most perfect expression of scorn."

"Some men see things as they are and ask why. Others dream things that never were and ask why not."

"Success does not consist in never making mistakes but in never making the same one a second time."

"Take care to get what you like or you will be forced to like what you get."

"That is the injustice of a woman's lot. A woman has to bring up her children; and that means to restrain them, to deny them things they want, to set them tasks, to punish them when they do wrong, to do all the unpleasant things. And then the father, who has nothing to do but pet them and spoil them, comes in when all her work is done and steals

"The average age (longevity) of a meat eater is 63. I am on the verge of 85 and still work as hard as ever. I have lived quite long enough and am trying to die; but I simply cannot do it. A single beef-steak would finish me; but I cannot bring myself to swallow it. I am oppressed with a dread of living forever. That is the only disadvantage of vegetarianism."

"The best place to seek God is in a garden. You can dig for him there."

"The best way to get your point across is to entertain."

"The difference between a lady and a flower girl is not how she behaves, but how she's treated."

"The fact that a believer is happier than a skeptic is no more to the point than the fact that a drunken man is happier than a sober one. The happiness of credulity is a cheap and dangerous quality of happiness, and by no means a necessity of life."

"The golden rule is that there are no golden rules."

"The liar's punishment is, not in the least that he is not believed, but that he cannot believe anyone else."

"The longer I live, the more I realize that I am never wrong about anything, and that all the pains I have so humbly taken to verify my notions have only wasted my time!"

"The man who writes about himself and his own time is the only man who writes about all people and all time."

"The man with toothache thinks everyone happy whose teeth are sound.

"The more I see of the moneyed classes, the more I understand the guillotine."

"The most tragic thing in the world is a man of genius who is not a man of honor."

"The only man I know who behaves sensibly is my tailor; he takes my measurements anew each time he sees me. The rest go on with their old measurements and expect me to fit them."

"The only service a friend can really render is to keep up your courage by holding up to you a mirror in which you can see a noble image of yourself."

"The only way to avoid being miserable is not to have enough leisure to wonder whether you are happy or not."

"The ordinary man is an anarchist. He wants to do as he likes. He may want his neighbor to be governed, but he himself doesn't want to be governed. He is mortally afraid of government officials and policemen."

"The people who get on in this world are the people who get up and look for the circumstances they want, and, if they can't find them, make them."

"The plain working truth is that it is not only good for people to be shocked occasionally, but absolutely necessary to the progress of society that they should be shocked pretty often."

"The play was a great success, but audience was a dismal failure."

"The power of accurate observation is commonly called cynicism by those who have not got it."

"The quality of a play is the quality of its ideas."

"The reasonable man adapts himself to the world: the unreasonable one persists in trying to adapt the world to himself. Therefore all progress depends on the unreasonable man."

"The schoolmaster is the person who takes the children off the parents' hands for a consideration. That is to say, he establishes a child prison, engages a number of employee schoolmasters as turnkeys, and covers up the essential cruelty and unnaturalness of the situation by torturing the children if they do not learn, and calling this process, which is within the capacity of any fool or blackguard, by the sacred name of Teaching."

"The secret of being miserable is to have leisure to bother about whether you are happy or not. The cure for it is occupation, because occupation means pre-occupation; and the pre-occupied person is neither happy nor unhappy, but simply alive and active. That is why it is necessary to happiness that one should be tired."

"The single biggest problem with communication is the illusion that it has taken place."

"The thought of two thousand people crunching celery at the same time horrified me."

"The trouble with her is that she lacks the power of conversation but not the power of speech."

"The word morality, if we met it in the Bible, would surprise us as much as the word telephone or motor car."

"The worst sin towards our fellow creatures is not to hate them, but to be indifferent to them; that's the essence of inhumanity."

"There are no secrets better kept than the secrets that everybody guesses."

"There is always danger for those who are afraid."

"There is no love sincerer than the love of food."

"There is no satisfaction in hanging a man who does not object to it."

"There is only one religion, though there are a hundred versions of it."

"There is, on the whole, nothing on earth intended for innocent people so horrible as a school. To begin with, it is a prison. But in some respects more cruel than a prison. In a prison, for instance, you are not forced to read books written by the warders and the governor. . . .In the prison you are not forced to sit listening to turnkeys discoursing without charm or interest on subjects that they don't understand and don't care about, and therefore incapable of making you understand or care about. In a prison they may torture your body; but they do not torture your brains."

"This is the true joy in life, the being used for a purpose recognized by yourself as a mighty one; the being thoroughly worn out before you are thrown on the scrap heap; the being a force of Nature instead of a feverish selfish little clod of ailments and grievances complaining that the world will not devote itself to making you happy."

"Those who cannot change their minds cannot change anything."

"Those who talk most about the blessings of marriage and the constancy of its vows are the very people who declare that if the chain were broken and the prisoners left free to choose, the whole social fabric would fly asunder. You cannot have the argument both ways. If the prisoner is happy, why lock him in? If he is not, why pretend that he is?"

"Thus, I blush to add, you can not be a philosopher and a good man, though you may be a philosopher and a great one."

"To be in hell is to drift; to be in heaven is to steer."

"Use your health, even to the point of wearing it out. That is what it is for. Spend all you have before you die; do not outlive yourself."

"War does not decide who is right but who is left."

"We are made wise not by the recollection of our past, but by the responsibility for our future."

"We cut the throat of a calf and hang it up by the heels to bleed to death so that our veal cutlet may be white; we nail geese to a board and cram them with food because we like the taste of liver disease; we tear birds to pieces to decorate our women's hats; we mutilate domestic animals for no reason at all except to follow an instinctively cruel fashion; and we connive at the most abominable tortures in the hope of discovering some magical cure for our own diseases by them."

"We don't stop playing because we grow old; we grow old because we stop playing."

"We have no more right to consume happiness without producing it than to consume wealth without producing it."

"We learn from experience that men never learn anything from experience."

"We should all be obliged to appear before a board every five years and justify our existence...on pain of liquidation"

"We're human beings we are - all of us - and that's what people are liable to forget. Human beings don't like peace and goodwill and everybody loving everybody else. However much they may think they do, they don't really because they're not made like that. Human beings love eating and drinking and loving and hating. They also like showing off, grabbing all they can, fighting for their rights and bossing anybody who'll give them half a chance."

"What is life but a series of inspired follies? The difficulty is to find them to do. Never lose a chance: it doesn't come every day."

"What is the matter with universities is that the students are school children, whereas it is of the very essence of university education that they should be adults."

"What we want to see is the child in pursuit of the knowledge not the knowledge in pursuit of the child."

"What you are to do without me I cannot imagine."

"When a man wants to murder a tiger he calls it sport; when a tiger wants to murder him he calls it ferocity."

"When a stupid man is doing something he is ashamed of, he always declares that it is his duty."

"When a thing is funny, search it carefully for a hidden truth."

"When the horrors of anarchy force us to set up laws that forbid us to fight and torture one another for sport, we still snatch at every excuse for declaring individuals outside the protection of law and torturing them to our hearts content."

"When two people are under the influence of the most violent, most insane, most delusive, and most transient of passions, they are required to swear that they will remain in that excited, abnormal, and exhausting condition continuously until death do them part."

"When you loved me I gave you the whole sun and stars to play with. I gave you eternity in a single moment, strength of the mountains in one clasp of your arms, and the volume of all the seas in one impulse of your soul."

"Which painting in the National Gallery would I save if there was a fire? The one nearest the door of course."

"While we ourselves are the living graves of murdered beasts, how can we expect any ideal conditions on this earth?"

"Why should we take advice on sex from the pope? If he knows anything about it, he shouldn't!"

"Without art, the crudeness of reality would make the world unbearable."

"Would the world ever have been made if its maker had been afraid of making trouble?Making life means making trouble. There's only one way of escaping trouble; and that's killing things."

"Written over the gate here are the words 'Leave every hope behind, ye who enter.' Only think what a relief that is! For what is hope? A form of moral responsibility. Here there is no hope, and consequently no duty, no work, nothing to be gained by praying, nothing to be lost by doing what you like. Hell, in short is a place where you have nothing to do but amuse yourself."

"You are going to let the fear of poverty govern your life and your reward will be that you will eat, but you will not live."

"You cannot have power for good without having power for evil too. Even mother's milk nourishes murderers as well as heroes."

"You don't stop laughing when you grow old, you grow old when you stop laughing."

"You have learnt something. That always feels at first as if you have lost something."

"You know well I couldn't bear to live with a low common man after you two; and it's wicked and cruel of you to insult me by pretending I could."

"You see things; you say, 'Why?' But I dream things that never were; and I say 'Why not?'"

"You use a glass mirror to see your face; you use works of art to see your soul."

41

"You'll never have a quiet world till you knock the patriotism out of the human race."

"Youth is wasted on the young."